Contents

Any words appearing in the text in bold,
like this, are explained in the Glossary.
You can also look out for them in the 'In the
know' box at the bottom of each page.

Fit and healthy

What do you think?

Everyone feels differently about sport. Take a look at these comments.

I hate games lessons.

I do loads of exercise, but I'm still fat.

All my friends are skinny, but I've got big hips.

I can't run far because I've got asthma.

Sport is boring.

To make the most out of life you need to be fit and healthy. If you are fit and healthy you are more likely to be able to do all the things you love doing, such as dancing with your friends, walking to school or to the shops and playing your favourite sports.

Keeping fit can help you live longer and help to prevent **diseases** in the future. It can help you to feel good about yourself and make your body strong and flexible. Exercise can also help you relax. There is only one person responsible for taking care of your body and keeping it healthy. That person is YOU.

How do I know if I am doing enough exercise?

asthma   condition that makes breathing difficult

Teen Issues

FITNESS

e to be returned on or before

Joanna Kedge and Joanna Watson

www.raintreepublishers.co.uk
Visit our website to find out more information about **Raintree** books.

To order:
 Phone 44 (0) 1865 888113
Send a fax to 44 (0) 1865 314091
Visit the Raintree Bookshop at **www.raintreepublishers.co.uk** to browse our catalogue and order online.

First published in Great Britain by
Raintree, Halley Court,
Jordan Hill, Oxford OX2 8EJ, part of
Harcourt Education.
Raintree is a registered trademark of Harcourt
Education Ltd.

© Harcourt Education Ltd 2004
First published in paperback in 2005
The moral right of the proprietor has been asserted.

Editorial: Charlotte Guillain
and Kate Buckingham
Design: Michelle Lisseter
and Tinstar Design Ltd (www.tinstar.co.uk)
Picture Research: Mica Brancic
Production: Jonathan Smith
Index: Indexing Specialists (UK) Ltd

Originated by Dot Gradations
Printed and bound in China by South China
Printing Company

ISBN 1 844 43145 2 (hardback)
08 07 06 05 04
10 9 8 7 6 5 4 3 2 1

ISBN 1 844 43152 5 (paperback)
09 08 07 06 05
10 9 8 7 6 5 4 3 2 1

British Library Cataloguing in Publication Data
Kedge, Joanna and Watson, Joanna
Fitness
613.7
A full catalogue record for this book is available from
the British Library.

Acknowledgements
The publishers would like to thank the following for
permission to reproduce photographs: Action Plus p.
39; Alamy pp. 10, 10–11, 11, 14, 29, 46–47; Anthony
Blake Picture Library p. 19; Australian Sports
Commission p. 12; BananaStock p. 30, 47 (Creatas);
Corbis pp. 5, 6, 8–9, 9, 18, 19, 21, 22–23, 25, 27, 29,
31, 32–33, 33, 34, 40–41, 41, 52–53; Getty p. 50;
Getty p. 28 (Imagebank); Getty pp. 4–5, 5, 5, 6–7, 8,
32, 32, 32, 42, 43, 48, 50–51 (Photodisc); Getty pp.
15, 23, 40, 48–49 (Taxi); John Birdsall pp. 24, 26, 37,
44, 45; Liz Eddison pp. 16, 34; Powerstock pp. 4, 22;
Rex Features p. 30–31; Robert Ashton pp. 13, 51;
Science Photo Library pp. 7, 12–13, 17, 17, 20, 20,
38; Steve J. Benbow p. 32; Stockfile p. 24 (S. Behr);
The Sport Library p. 16; Trevor Clifford p. 16; Tudor
Photography pp. i, 36, 36, 36–37, 37, 37, 39, 46.

Cover photo of a pair of trainers reproduced with
permission of Robert Harding Picture Library.

Every effort has been made to contact copyright
holders of any material reproduced in this book. Any
omissions will be rectified in subsequent printings if
notice is given to the publishers.

Fit for what?

When you say the word 'fit' lots of people think of top sports people winning medals for their country. Sports people like this train every day and being fit is part of their job. They need to be super fit to be able to compete and win.

However, the sort of fitness that we are talking about is for everyone. People like you, and your friends and family. It is about keeping healthy and having fun.

What do we think about our bodies?

How can you fit exercise into your life?

How can exercise help you make friends?

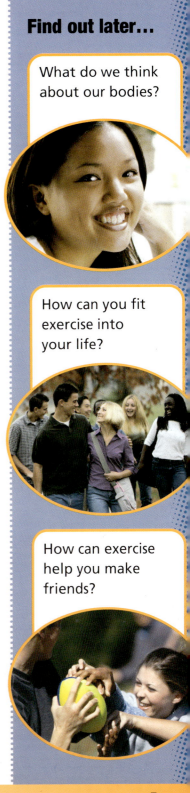

Why am I no good at sport?

How do I lose weight?

Why do people keep fit?

There are loads of reasons why people keep fit. Sometimes they want to be fit to play sport and be in a team. Or they want to feel better about the way they look. They know that keeping fit can help them to lose weight and look **toned**.

professional   doing something as a job, not just as a hobby

It is not just about looking good though. Some people do regular exercise to keep their insides healthy too. Exercise is great for your heart, lungs, muscles and bones. Lots of young people also play sport or do exercise like rollerblading or skateboarding because they are enjoyable and a good way of making friends.

I want to be a **professional** footballer, so I have to train hard.

I get really **stressed** about school work and exams. Keeping fit makes me feel better. It helps me to relax and sleep well.

I love doing exercise with my friends. It's great fun and we have a real laugh.

Heart

There are so many benefits of doing regular exercise. It can mean the difference between life and death.

▼ The heart on the left is **diseased**. It is the heart of a person who has done little exercise and eaten unhealthy foods. The heart on the right is from a healthy person who has exercised regularly.

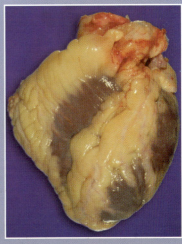

stressed feeling pressured about something
toned muscles are tight and move easily

Why do you keep fit?

Keep fit, have fun

Are you bored in the evenings? Fed up of watching TV? Why not join a sports club or go to an exercise class? It is a great way of meeting new people and making friends.

I used to hate swimming when I was younger. I remember getting cold and having wet hair dripping down my back. Yuck. But about a year ago I joined a swimming club and now I love it. I go twice a week and I've made loads of new friends. It's made me feel really healthy and I always feel **energetic** on swimming nights. On a Friday night after swimming, we all go dancing and have a real laugh. I can't imagine my week without swimming and my new friends any more.

energetic   full of life and not easily tired

'Keeping fit helps you lose weight.'

TRUE

A combination of healthy eating and exercise will help you to keep at a weight that you are happy with. Doing regular exercise increases your **metabolism** so your body stores less of the food you eat as fat. It also builds up your muscles, making your body feel more **toned** and shapely.

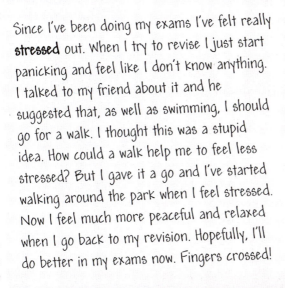

Since I've been doing my exams I've felt really **stressed** out. When I try to revise I just start panicking and feel like I don't know anything. I talked to my friend about it and he suggested that, as well as swimming, I should go for a walk. I thought this was a stupid idea. How could a walk help me to feel less stressed? But I gave it a go and I've started walking around the park when I feel stressed. Now I feel much more peaceful and relaxed when I go back to my revision. Hopefully, I'll do better in my exams now. Fingers crossed!

Body changes

Our bodies change as we get older. If you think back to what you were like as a young child, you will see how much your body has changed already. Between the ages of nine and sixteen, all young people go through some very big changes.

Here are some young people's thoughts on some of these body changes.

I felt so embarrassed when my breasts first started showing. All the girls were comparing how big they were. Some of my friends had breasts much earlier than me and other friends still haven't developed any. Once you know that everyone else is going through these changes too, it becomes easier.

I felt really embarrassed when my breasts started growing and I had to wear a bra. I know it is normal though.

Even though I did lots of exercise, when I went through puberty I put weight on and my hips got wider.

hormones   chemical messengers that are released by the brain and sent around the body

These changes will happen to different people at different times, but eventually everyone will go through them. This time in a young person's life is called **puberty**. It begins when chemicals called **hormones** are released into the brain. The main female hormone is called oestrogen and the male hormone is called testosterone.

> I seem to get more sweaty now. I need to wash more and wear deodorant.

> My friend Peter started growing small breasts at the start of puberty, but they soon went away.

Spot alert

Even though I know the changes are natural and it's all just a part of me growing up, I hate getting spots. My skin is much oilier than it used to be and I have to keep it cleaner. I wash my face, shoulders and chest at least twice a day to keep my spots under control.

puberty   changes that happen to young people as they grow into adults

Why exercise?

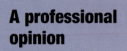

A professional opinion

Keeping fit and exercising helps us in different ways. It makes us stronger and increases our **stamina**, which means that we can keep going for longer. Exercise also improves our flexibility, making it easier for us to touch our toes or reach for things on a high shelf. It also gives us more energy.

A strong heart and lungs provide a sure path to living a longer and more enjoyable life. Playing sport is not only good for your health, but gives you the chance to make friends. Through sport I have travelled the world and seen many new and exciting things.

Tudor Bidder, Olympic coach

endorphins   natural drugs made in the brain that make you feel happy and good about yourself

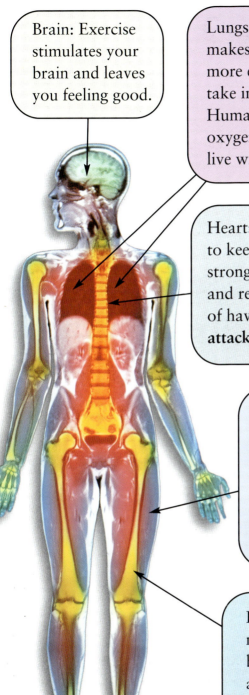

Brain: Exercise stimulates your brain and leaves you feeling good.

Lungs: Exercise makes you breathe more efficiently and take in more **oxygen**. Humans need oxygen – we cannot live without it.

Heart: Exercise helps to keep your heart strong and healthy and reduces the risk of having a **heart attack** or **stroke**.

Muscles: Exercise strengthens your muscles and makes them more flexible.

Bones: Exercise makes your bones stronger and less likely to break if you fall over.

Energy

Exercise stimulates your brain to make natural body chemicals called **endorphins**. This is what leaves you feeling energized after a good workout.

Benefits to muscles

Healthy muscles are not just important for sportspeople. Muscles are the parts of your body that help you to move. They are usually fixed to the bones in your body by **tendons**. When we want to walk or move, messages from the brain tell the muscles how they should work. If you exercise regularly, your muscles will become stronger and more **supple**. By exercising your muscles, your body stores less fat, so you will stay in good shape too.

Too much muscle

I thought I would look so cool, having a huge chest and big arm muscles, but instead I look like a freak. If only I had listened to all my friends telling me that it was dangerous for my health to work out on just one area of my body.

▶ This girl is doing a spinal twist stretch in a yoga class.

qualified   having the correct training
supple   easy to bend

Q & A

Dear Doc,
I know that exercise is really good for my body and muscles, but I don't want my muscles to get too big in some places, like my legs and arms. What exercise can I do that would be good for my whole body?

From Emma, age 14

Q What sort of exercise is good for all my muscles?

A Dancing, yoga or swimming are all fantastic ways to build and strengthen all the muscles in your body at the same time.

Dear Emma,
You are right that exercise is good for you, but it is a bad idea to focus too much on certain muscles. The best type of exercise gives you an all-over workout, so that all your muscles are fit and healthy. Swimming is really good, and yoga is excellent for general fitness too. Make sure that before deciding what to do you get good advice from a teacher or other **qualified** person.

tendons very strong bands of tissue that connect your muscles to your bones

Heart beat

Did you know that your heart beats 100,000 times each day and that a healthy heart never gets tired?

Recipe for a healthy heart:

- eat at least five portions of fruit and vegetables every day

- do at least three sessions of exercise each week

- never start smoking.

Benefits to the heart

Exercising gets your circulation working well, which makes your heart stronger. The best type of exercise for your heart is **aerobic** exercise, which allows more blood and **oxygen** to be pumped around the body. Popular aerobic activities include fast walking, jogging, swimming, cycling and dancing. Being overweight or **obese** can put a strain on your heart and cause it to stop working properly. Being overweight as a teenager can have serious effects on your health for the rest of your life. It is easy to start solving the problem by doing some simple exercise.

cholesterol   fatty substance made by the body that can block the arteries to and from the heart

Sometimes I really hate myself for being fat. I get tired just walking up the stairs or going to the local shops. My doctor says I'm putting pressure on my heart. If I'm not more careful, I will be seriously ill before I'm even twenty. She told me to find an exercise that I enjoy, even if I just dance to music at home sometimes. She also thinks I should eat more fruit and vegetables and fewer chips and fried fatty foods. I'm going to really try to lose weight. I want to join in with other people my age, and know that I'm healthy.

Why can't I eat lots of fatty foods?

The **arteries** in our body carry food and oxygen in the blood. Eating foods that contain a lot of fat and **cholesterol**, like chips and burgers, can block up the arteries. Many people have **heart attacks** and other heart-related problems because of blocked arteries.

▶ ▶ ▶ ▶ ▶ ▶

Try the quiz on pages 26 to 27 to see how you feel about your body.

obese   very overweight

Q I love sport but my knees hurt when I run or play on hard surfaces like concrete. Is it better for me to play on grass?

A Exercise should be done on soft surfaces when possible. Otherwise, the impact of the ground on your joints, like your knees, ankles and hips, is too strong and may damage them. Keep to the grass when you can and do lots of different sports.

▶ The best way to avoid osteoporosis is to do lots of exercise when you are younger.

Benefits to bones

Our skeletons are the frameworks that hold our bodies together. So we need to look after our bones – a great way to do that is to exercise. Young children have very **supple** and soft bones. You may have noticed that even though very young children fall over a lot, they seem to bounce and not hurt themselves too seriously. This is because their bones are springy so they bend rather than break.

Some elderly people develop a **disease** called **osteoporosis**, which means that their bones become very thin and weak, so they can break easily.

calcium   mineral that is essential for healthy growth of bones and teeth

What sort of exercise is good for my bones?

As we get older our bones become harder and more **brittle**. Any sort of exercise is good for us, but sports and games played on the ground, such as jogging, football, netball and baseball are especially good for bones.

These types of exercise are called weight-bearing because you are carrying the weight of your own body. **Weight-bearing exercises** stimulate the bones to grow, which means they become thicker and stronger and are less likely to break. Whenever possible though, you should exercise on grass or soft surfaces, otherwise these sorts of exercises can damage the joints between the bones and cause a lot of pain.

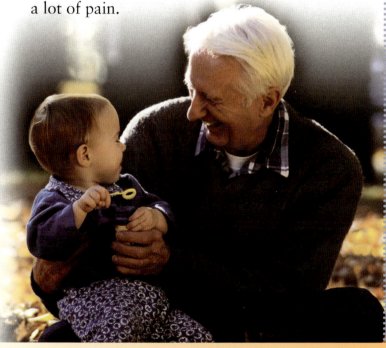

A healthy diet

▲ There is lots of calcium in foods like milk, yoghurt and cheese.

Food is really important for keeping healthy too. To make sure that your bones are strong and can grow healthily try to eat a **balanced diet**, including lots of foods rich in **calcium**. Calcium is a **mineral** that helps bones and teeth grow.

mineral   simple substance found naturally in the Earth
osteoporosis   condition that makes bones brittle and fragile

Benefits to lungs

We all breathe without even having to think about it. Have you noticed that your breathing gets faster after you have been running or doing exercise? This is because your body needs extra **oxygen** to feed the muscles that are working harder. We need oxygen to **survive**, just like we need food and water. When we get energy from food we make a waste material called **carbon dioxide** which our body needs to get rid of. It does this by breathing out. So we breathe oxygen in, and carbon dioxide out. Exercising makes our lung capacity bigger which means that we can get rid of the carbon dioxide more quickly.

Look after your lungs

Tobacco contains a drug called **nicotine**, as well as other chemicals. These chemicals can cause cancer, which can result in death. Smoking also makes the lungs dirty so they do not work as well, causing heart and lung **disease**.

▼ The lung on the left is a healthy lung. The lung on the right is covered in black dots. This is **tar** from cigarettes.

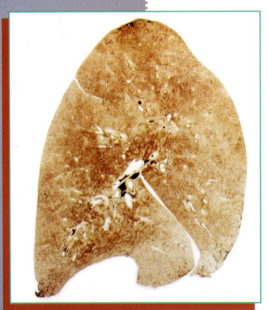
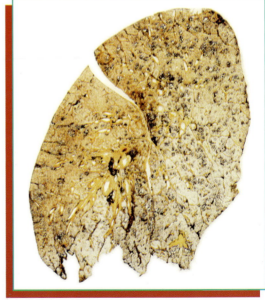

nicotine   poisonous drug found in tobacco

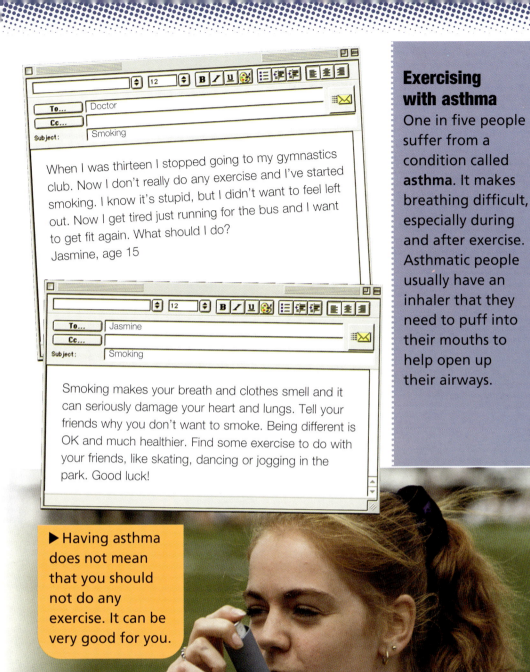

To... Doctor
Cc...
Subject: Smoking

When I was thirteen I stopped going to my gymnastics club. Now I don't really do any exercise and I've started smoking. I know it's stupid, but I didn't want to feel left out. Now I get tired just running for the bus and I want to get fit again. What should I do?
Jasmine, age 15

To... Jasmine
Cc...
Subject: Smoking

Smoking makes your breath and clothes smell and it can seriously damage your heart and lungs. Tell your friends why you don't want to smoke. Being different is OK and much healthier. Find some exercise to do with your friends, like skating, dancing or jogging in the park. Good luck!

▶ Having asthma does not mean that you should not do any exercise. It can be very good for you.

Exercising with asthma

One in five people suffer from a condition called **asthma**. It makes breathing difficult, especially during and after exercise. Asthmatic people usually have an inhaler that they need to puff into their mouths to help open up their airways.

Confidence and energy

Kelly's journal

Q I always feel fat in my sports kit and it means that I never want to do sports at school. Do you have any suggestions?

A It is sometimes really difficult if you feel **negative** about your body. How about trying some exercise at the weekends with family or friends. That way you will slowly get fit and feel better about yourself.

About four years ago, I felt really fed up with my life. I had just changed school and I am quite shy, so I was finding it difficult to make new friends. Also, my body was changing a lot as I got older and I had started putting on weight. The more down I felt, the harder it was to cheer myself up and I would just sit around feeling tired and lonely.

Even though I do lots of exercise, I have more energy now than I have ever had.

confident   sure and certain about what you are doing

Then, someone talked me into going to a basketball game. I didn't want to play at first, but nobody was really that good, so I gave it a try and now I love it. It was good because I could talk to the other girls about the game and soon I made some friends. Now I can go out to the park with them and just have a laugh. I feel fit too, so I have stopped worrying about my body.

Get groovin'

We love going out dancing. It's great exercise and makes us feel good about our bodies.

Yeah, it's good to do exercise with someone — it's more fun. Get out there dancing or skateboarding with a friend.

Practising basketball and getting better at it makes me feel much more **confident** and positive about myself.

Stress relief and relaxation

Feeling the strain

How are you feeling about the dreaded exams? I'm so worried that I can't even sleep.

I know the feeling exactly. I joined the local running club and I feel so much better. Maybe you should try some exercise too?

Monday June 7

Mum and Dad are on holiday. Grandma is staying to keep an eye on us. My brother is annoying me. He doesn't do anything around the house to help me and grandma out. I decided to go for a bike ride instead of shouting at him. It must have helped because when I got home I felt really relaxed and was able to concentrate on my homework better. I must remember that trick next time I'm **stressed**.

tension   feeling worried and unable to relax

Take your mind off it

Sometimes life can feel tough and stressful. Everyone has times when they feel like they cannot cope with everything they have to do. Exercise is a fantastic way of making yourself feel better. It can ease **tension** and stress and leave you feeling good inside. This is because exercise releases special chemicals in the brain called **endorphins** which make you feel peaceful and relaxed. Regular exercise also helps you to sleep better which gives you more energy for the next day.

How you relax

It's fun to sit and chat.

Since joining the hockey team, I feel a lot less stressed about my school work.

I go to a yoga class. It's great for relaxation.

25

Body thoughts

Looking good

> I want to look good for me, not for anyone else.

> Yeah, I would rather be fit and healthy than look like some sort of skinny model.

What do you think of yourself? For each question, write down a, b, or c and check out what your answers say about your image of yourself.

To be healthy, you need to:
a) have a laugh with your friends
b) eat good food and do some exercise
c) look great.

Exercise is great because:
a) I never do it
b) you can play sport with your friends and feel fit and healthy
c) it gives me a perfect body.

What is your idea of a perfect day?
a) lying on the sofa, eating and watching TV
b) being out with friends, playing sport in the park
c) trying on new outfits and looking at yourself in the mirror.

How did you score?

Now, count up the number of 'a's, 'b's and 'c's you have.

Mostly a: You risk becoming a slob. You really do need to take a bit more care of your **appearance** and look after your health. How about playing some sport at the weekend or walking to school to give you some energy?

Mostly b: You have a healthy outlook on life. You take regular exercise and it seems that you think your friends are more important than your looks.

Mostly c: You may be a little **obsessed** with the way you look. Remember that it is far more important to be fit and healthy on the inside than to look 'perfect' on the outside. How about going out and playing some sport and not worrying so much about your looks?

Puberty

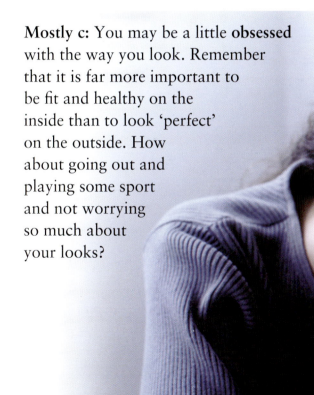

Sometimes **puberty** felt like a nightmare. I was so aware of my body and all the changes that were happening to it. I felt more shy and self-conscious. But once my friends and I realized that we all felt a bit freaked out by it and that it was normal, everyone relaxed.

---

obsessed   think about something all the time

Exercise addiction

We all know how good exercise is for us. It makes us feel good about ourselves and it helps us to control our weight. Some people go on diets and others exercise to achieve their **ideal weight** and fitness level. Sensible eating and exercising are the way to do this, but some people become addicted and diet and exercise too much. As a result they often become ill. Remember, your body needs activity but it also needs rest.

Are you an addict?

Do you, or your friend:

- Force yourself to exercise, even if you do not feel well?

- Prefer to exercise rather than be with friends?

- Worry that you will gain weight if you skip exercising for a day?

- Feel worried if you miss a workout?

If you answered 'yes' to any of these questions, try talking to someone you trust – you may have an exercise **addiction**.

addiction   when you cannot stop doing something

Addicted Athlete

A teenage athlete collapsed during yesterday's race after months of tough training. Sunita, age 15, had exercised twice a day leading up to the big race. She even trained when she was unwell and in the pouring rain. Her body finally gave in during the race, when she couldn't even reach the finishing line. Sunita is now resting at home and admits, 'I've learned my lesson. Exercising took over my life. What happened has made me realise that I need to make time for other things, like my friends and family. I need to take care of my body rather than exhaust it.'

Using performance-enhancing drugs

No thanks

Dear Doctor,
I play volleyball with a team of friends. Some of my mates have started talking about using steroids to make us play better. What should I do?
Jake, 15

To... Doctor
Cc...
Subject: Steroids

To... Jake
Cc...
Subject: Steroids

Steroids can cause heart disease, panic attacks and even breast growth in boys. Explain to your friends why you don't want to take any and give them some information about the dangers. Ask them to come and see me for a chat too.

Most athletes and sportspeople rely on talent and hard training to get the results they want, but some try and cheat by using drugs to enhance their performance. The most common drugs are **anabolic steroids**. They are sometimes given names such as 'roids', 'juice', 'hype' or 'pump'. They work by allowing the body to do much heavier training and recover more quickly than is naturally possible. They act like the male **hormone** testosterone and are often used as a shortcut to training for long-distance runners and wrestlers. Their use is against the law and most championships, like the Olympics, have banned them.

▶ Paula Radcliffe running in the 2003 London Marathon.

acne   collection of spots, pimples and blackheads on the face, shoulders and chest

The use of steroids is unfair on those athletes who have trained hard and improved their performance naturally. Steroids can also have very serious effects on the body. These include:

- high **blood pressure** and heart **disease**
- liver damage and cancers
- headaches, aching joints and muscle **cramps**
- very serious aggressive behaviour
- anxiety and panic attacks
- very heavy **acne** on the face and back
- increase in the size of breasts for boys and men
- decrease in the size of breasts for girls and women
- problems with periods in girls and women.

Did you know?

- Some steroids can be safe when prescribed by a doctor for an illness or condition? These will not affect performance at all.

- Performance-enhancing steroids could make both boys and girls go bald?

❝ Using drugs in sport is a criminal offence and should be treated as such. It not only cheats other athletes, but also promoters, sponsors and the general public. ❞

Paula Radcliffe,
Olympic athlete

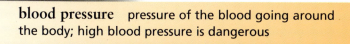

blood pressure   pressure of the blood going around the body; high blood pressure is dangerous

What do you think?

People who use steroids are cheats. Taking steroids is illegal, anyway.

Steroids are drugs.

All sports people should be tested for drugs.

Why should some people take them and others not? It's not fair.

Interview with an athlete who has chosen not to be named

Q How many gold medals have you won?

A Six, but the last one didn't count.

Q Were you very disappointed when you were **disqualified** from the race?

A Of course I was. I've been training for months for this big competition. I've only been taking the **anabolic steroids** for one month and I didn't think anyone would find out. I wish I hadn't taken them because I probably would have won anyway.

Q Why did you take them then?

A I know a few other athletes who take them and they encouraged me. I didn't think I would have a chance if they were taking them and I wasn't.

▶ Ben Johnson won the 100 metre race at the 1988 Olympics. The gold medal was later taken away from him when it was revealed he had been using steroids.

disqualified   dismissed from a competition

Q How did the anabolic steroids make you feel?

A Sometimes I felt stronger and faster. But I got spots all over my face and back and I became very aggressive. I had really bad headaches and **cramps**. I have a very high **blood pressure** now and my liver may be damaged. The most embarrassing thing is that I've started to develop breasts.

Q So, would you ever take them again?

A I would never take them again. I've missed out on a gold medal and I have seriously damaged my body. Hopefully I can get myself back to normal, but the damage to my heart and liver won't go away.

Magazines and the media sometimes push people to take steroids but there are so many risks that it would be silly to take them.

Taking care of your body

When we exercise we use lots of energy because our muscles work harder than when we rest. So, we need to feed those muscles with really healthy food to make them work properly.

To get the best out of our bodies, we have to feed them the best sorts of **fuel**.

The food pyramid opposite shows how much of each type of food we should eat. The foods at the top of the pyramid should be eaten the least. The foods at the bottom you should try and eat the most of.

I always try to eat well – loads of fruit and veg and other healthy stuff to give me a **balanced diet**. I know this gives me my best performance. The night before a competition, I always eat a huge bowl of spaghetti and make sure I have got a bunch of bananas in my bag.

Recipe

Why not get an energy kick from this Banana Smoothie. All you need is:

- 1 banana, half a glass of unsweetened fruit juice and any other fruit that you like.

All you need to do is:

- mash up the banana with a fork or in a blender
- add the fruit juice and mix in
- add any other fruit and mash this in
- stir and drink your delicious smoothie.

Fruit and vegetables: These contain lots of vitamins and **minerals** and are essential to stay healthy and fit. They help prevent the body from catching illnesses, they clean our blood and they make our teeth, nerves, skin and bones healthy too. It is recommended that we all eat at least five portions of fresh fruit and vegetables every day. Count how many you have had so far today.

Fats and sugars: These foods should be eaten as little as possible because they can make our body fat, block up our **arteries** and rot our teeth.

Protein: These are foods that help to build muscle and repair the body. These foods include fish, meat, nuts, pulses and eggs.

Carbohydrates: These are starchy foods that give your body energy. These foods include pasta, rice, bread and potatoes.

Warming up and cooling down

It is very important to do some **warm up** stretching exercises before you begin a session of sport or physical activity. Some people think it is a waste of time, but it helps to stop you getting injured.

Some good ways of warming up your muscles are walking, cycling, jogging and dancing. Stretches should also be a part of warming up. **Professional** athletes always stretch and loosen up before their event. Here are some of the stretches they might do.

Stand with your feet apart. Bend one knee while keeping the other straight. Bend until a stretch is felt down the inner thigh. Can you feel the stretch? Swap legs.

With one hand on a wall, grasp the ankle with the other hand so that your foot is pulled up towards your bottom. Can you feel the stretch? Swap legs.

warm down   allows the body to gradually return to its normal activity levels

Stand with your feet hip-width apart. Lift one arm above your head and lean over to one side. Can you feel the stretch? Swap arms.

Stand with your feet hip-width apart and your hands on your hips. Lean forward until your body is parallel with the floor. Can you feel the stretch?

Why warm up and down?

- Warming up before exercise only takes 5 to 10 minutes.

- It is important to warm up before you exercise and to **warm down** afterwards.

- Stretching before and after exercise helps keep your muscles healthy.

Once I forgot to warm up before I went for a run and I hurt my knee.

warm up   gradually more energetic activities that safely prepare the body for exercise

Dealing with injuries

Collision

It is important to warm up before exercising and remember your limits, especially when you are playing a **contact sport**.

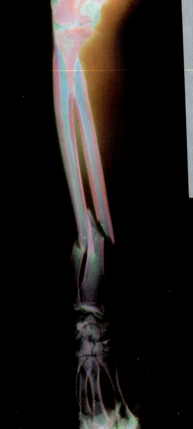

My name is Lola and I work as a **physiotherapist**, looking after people who have sports' injuries. So many of the people I treat have started doing some exercise but have not thought about how to do it safely. Often they do not understand how important it is to **warm up** before exercise and **warm down** afterwards. I always try to explain to patients that the fittest athletes in the world make sure that they warm up and down before and after exercise because they know it is not worth taking short cuts.

Some of the injuries are horrific. One teenager I treated had torn the **ligament** across his knee when he was tackled in a football game. He thought he was fit and hadn't bothered to warm up before playing. Ligaments are like rubber bands and the warmer they are, the more likely they are to stretch. This boy was in agony and had to have a cast put on his leg. It took him several months to recover – think of all that sport that he missed out on.

◀ This X-ray shows a nasty injury that happened when a basketball player took too many chances. She collided with another player and broke her arm.

ligament   strong but slightly stretchy material that holds joints together

Clubs lose £40m a year to injury

Injuries to footballers in England cost the game £40 million each season. More could be done to prevent this if players were better trained and coaches made more aware of sports medicine.

The *British Journal of Sports Medicine* says that managers and coaches are putting pressure on players to play even while they are injured.

REMEMBER: If you do have any pain when you are exercising you should stop at once. If the pain continues, go to your doctor. You may be sent to a physiotherapist who can sort out the problem or give you simple exercises that will make you feel better.

How much exercise?

How much is too much?

This boy is doing too much exercise in a week. He should not be exercising more than once a day.

I've been going running for two years now. I love it. I go nearly every day, even when it's freezing cold or raining. I go swimming quite a lot too. I worry a lot about my weight and would love to be a model. I love my food you see, so I feel that if I do loads of exercise I can eat more. Sometimes my friends get annoyed with me because they think I would rather be exercising than seeing them. That isn't true, but I do feel awful if I miss my daily run or swim. They just don't understand.

Monday: a.m. went for a run,
               p.m. football training
Tuesday: a.m. swim,
               p.m. gym session
Wednesday: p.m. football training
Thursday: a.m. went for a run,
               p.m. swim
Friday: a.m. gym session
Saturday: a.m. football training
Sunday: a.m. two hour gym session

I wonder if I do enough exercise.

Exercising three times a week for at least half an hour is a good way to improve your health. The body's joints can be damaged by too much heavy exercise. These are called 'over-use' injuries. It is important to make time for other things too, like your friends and school work.

All she ever does is exercise and worry about the way she looks. She's so boring these days and seems to have forgotten about her friends. If she's not careful, she won't have any left. We all exercise too, but only about three times a week. That way we have the time and energy to do other things.

Top tip
You can build up to going for a jog by starting off with a brisk walk. After about two weeks of walking you could try speeding up into a run.

▼ Start off slowly. Gradually build up to a jog as you get fitter.

Make it fun

Some useful ideas to help you have fun keeping fit:

- exercise with a friend
- choose something you enjoy
- remember, dancing is exercise too
- above all, have fun!

Building fitness into your life

Do you love being active or is it your idea of a nightmare? There is only one way to find out.

Write down a, b or c for each question, then add up your score at the end.

How do you get to school?
a) walk
b) car
c) bus.

If you had the choice, would you:
a) use the stairs
b) get in a lift
c) use the escalator.

How often do you exercise?
a) three times a week
b) once a year
c) once a week.

Which statement best describes you?
a) I really love being active
b) I hate all types of physical activity
c) I don't mind physical activity if my friends are doing it with me.

How did you score?

Add up how many 'a's, 'b's and 'c's you have and find out if you need to change your lifestyle to be more active.

Mostly a: You are very fit and active. Keep up the good work.

Mostly b: You need to try to fit more exercise into your week. Find something you enjoy and try to work towards exercising three times a week.

Mostly c: You like exercising with your friends so find things that you can do together like dancing, skateboarding, rollerblading or cycling.

Q & A

Q I am so busy with school work and seeing my mates, I don't have time to exercise. What can I do to keep fit?

A Why don't you go out dancing with your friends. Or how about walking to school or to your mates' houses instead of getting a lift or the bus?

A little bit everyday

My name is Shandip. Two years ago, I was really struggling to do any exercise. Then I realized that there were lots of ways to get fit. Now I walk to school and cycle with friends and I'm fit. A little extra effort has made all the difference.

Top Ten Tips

Exercise is not just about athletics or playing a sport. Look at our experts' ideas for how to fit fitness into your day:

- When visiting a friend, why not cycle there?

- Going for a fast walk in the fresh air is great exercise.

- Helping your parents with heavy bags of shopping will help tone your arm muscles.

- Walking with a friend rather than catching the bus to school will help you burn a few more calories.

- Gardening is a great way of exercising. Ask your neighbours if they have any odd jobs for you to do.

- Even helping out with the housework at home can be good for you.

- How about getting off the bus or train one stop early so that you can walk the extra distance?

- Instead of using a lift or escalator, why not use the stairs?

- How about going for a walk at lunchtime?

- Have you got a bike? How about cycling to the shops?

calorie   measures the energy value of food

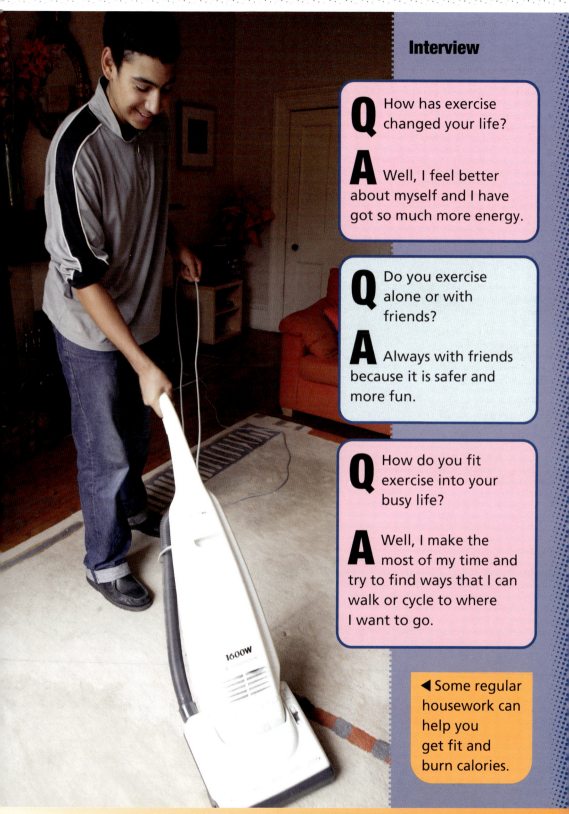

Q How has exercise changed your life?

A Well, I feel better about myself and I have got so much more energy.

Q Do you exercise alone or with friends?

A Always with friends because it is safer and more fun.

Q How do you fit exercise into your busy life?

A Well, I make the most of my time and try to find ways that I can walk or cycle to where I want to go.

◄ Some regular housework can help you get fit and burn calories.

Easy and cheap sports

Fit and free

Rollerblading was great fun i feel full of energy now.

abc 424/1
i loved it 2. Lets do it again soon

There are so many ways of exercising and everyone likes different things. Some people hate team sports and sports lessons. Some people hate doing exercise outside or on their own. But don't worry because whatever your choice is, there is something to suit everyone.

Why not try...

Exercise classes: These are usually done to music and are a good form of **aerobic** exercise. Find a class you enjoy. Why not go along with a friend?

Walking: Walking is great exercise, especially fast walking. You can do it anywhere too.

Team games like basketball, hockey, netball, football: Join a local club or team to play your favourite sport. It is a great way of making new friends as well as improving your fitness.

Cycling: Find a park that you are allowed to cycle in and enjoy the fresh air as well as the exercise.

Swimming: Swimming exercises so many different muscles and is great in the summer. It is cheap too.

Rollerblading: Go to a rollerblade park near you and enjoy having fun with your friends.

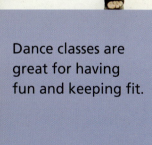

Dance classes are great for having fun and keeping fit.

Exercise with friends

So many benefits...

I've made new friends at my sports club.

I've lost weight and feel great since I started exercising more.

Remember, dancing is exercise too.

Above all, make sure exercise is fun.

'Get your sports kit on, it's time for games', our sports teacher used to shout at us. This was the time of week I hated most. Getting into those horrible shorts and top in the freezing cold just to run around the school field chasing a ball – not my idea of fun. I was pleased when I left school and didn't have to do sport and exercise anymore. But, after a year or so, I started to put on weight. All my clothes felt tight and I didn't have any energy to do anything anymore.

Exercise doesn't have to be painful.

It's a great way to hang out with friends and have some fun too.

Some of my friends started going to an **aerobics** class – I didn't like the sound of it but they told me it was great fun and eventually persuaded me to go with them. I'm glad I did, it was brilliant fun. The music was so cool and we had a real laugh – especially when we got the moves wrong and went in the wrong direction. I go every week now, sometimes twice a week. I can fit into all my clothes again because I have lost weight and my energy for life has returned. You should try it too.

◄ ◄ ◄ ◄ ◄
Turn to pages 36 and 37 to find out how to **warm up** before exercise.

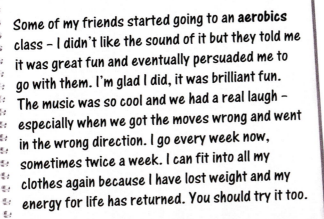

Cycling

Cycling can be energizing and really rewarding – especially if you reach the top of that hill!

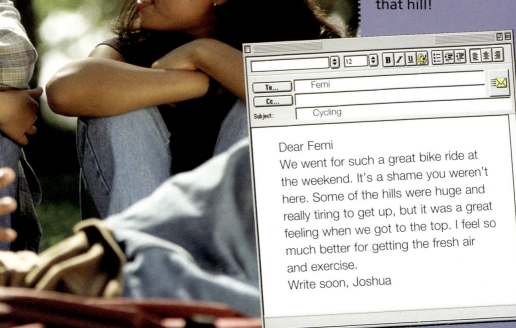

To... Femi
Cc...
Subject: Cycling

Dear Femi
We went for such a great bike ride at the weekend. It's a shame you weren't here. Some of the hills were huge and really tiring to get up, but it was a great feeling when we got to the top. I feel so much better for getting the fresh air and exercise.
Write soon, Joshua

Body and mind

Feeling great

I feel great about myself. I am fit and healthy on the inside and the outside. I have loads of fun exercising with friends and it makes me feel full of life.

Exercise can be lots of fun and is really important to keep your body and mind healthy. There are many ways of keeping fit and there is something to suit everyone. Some people like sports and **competitive** games, others prefer to do exercise as part of their everyday routine. It is up to you what you choose, but remember to make sure it is fun and enjoy it.

There are different types of exercise to suit everyone.

competitive   when one person or team wants to do better than the other

By exercising three times a week you will be well on your way to being fit and healthy. Remember that exercise is not only good for the way you look, but it also affects how you feel. And at the same time it will be keeping your bones, muscles, heart and lungs in great shape too. It is the best way to look after yourself.

Exercise can be cheap.

Don't forget that exercise is fun.

Surfing

If you live by the sea, try taking some surfing lessons. It is a great way to burn **calories**!

This is so cool.

Find out more

Organizations

Australian Council for Health, Physical Education and Recreation
A website promoting healthy lifestyles and physical education.
www.achper.org.au

Body and Mind
An interesting and easy-to-use website recommending ways to make our bodies and minds healthier.
www.bam.gov

BBC Health
A comprehensive guide to fitness, including ideas about how to get motivated and stay active.
www.bbc.co.uk/ health/fitness/

Lifebytes
A fun and informative website that gives young people information to help them make their own choices about life.
www.lifebytes.gov.uk

Books

Body Focus: Muscles, Carol Ballard (Heinemann Library, 2003)

Essential Sports: Basketball, Andy Smith (Heinemann Library, 2003)

Essential Sports: Football, Andy Smith (Heinemann Library, 2003)

Need to know: Steroids, Rob Alcraft (Heinemann Library, 2001)

World Wide Web

If you want to find out more about **fitness**, you can search the Internet using keywords like these:

• 'balanced diet'
• contact + sport
• aerobics
• ideal + weight

You can also find your own keywords by using headings or words from this book. Use the search tips opposite to help you find the most useful websites.

Search tips

There are billions of pages on the Internet so it can be difficult to find exactly what you are looking for. For example, if you just type in 'fitness' on a search engine like Google, you'll get a list of 25 million web pages. These search skills will help you find useful websites more quickly:

- Know exactly what you want to find out about first
- Use simple keywords instead of whole sentences
- Use two to six keywords in a search, putting the most important words first
- Be precise – only use names of people, places or things
- If you want to find words that go together, put quote marks around them, for example 'balanced diet' or 'ideal weight'
- Use the advanced section of your search engine.

Where to search

Search engine

A search engine looks through the web and lists the sites that match the words in the search box. They can give thousands of links, but the best matches are at the top of the list, on the first page. Try searching with **www.bbc.co.uk/ search**

Search directory

A search directory is like a library of websites. You can search by keyword or subject and browse through the different sites like you would look through books on a library shelf. A good example is **www.yahooligans. com**

Glossary

acne collection of spots, pimples and blackheads on the face, shoulders and chest`

addiction when you cannot stop doing something

aerobic exercise that strengthens the heart and lungs by pumping more oxygen and blood around the body

anabolic steroids illegal drugs that build body tissue

appearance the way you look

artery tube carrying blood from the heart to other parts of the body

asthma condition that makes breathing difficult

balanced diet eating a good range and mixture of foods from all the different food groups

blood pressure pressure of the blood going around the body; high blood pressure is dangerous

brittle easy to break

calcium mineral that is essential for healthy growth of bones and teeth

calorie measures the energy value of food

carbon dioxide gas found in the air. Plants use it when making food and both plants and animals give it off when they breathe out.

cholesterol fatty substance made by the body that can block the arteries to and from the heart, causing heart disease

competitive when one person or team wants to do better than the other

confident sure and certain about what you are doing

contact sport sport where physical contact between the players is either an essential part of the game, like rugby, or permitted within limits, like football

cramp sudden painful tightening of a muscle

disease unhealthy condition

disqualified dismissed from a competition

endorphins natural drugs made in the brain that make you feel happy and good about yourself

energetic full of life and not easily tired

fuel source of energy

heart attack sudden failure of the heart

hormones chemical messengers that are released by the brain and sent around the body

ideal weight best weight for your body, not anyone else's

ligament strong but slightly stretchy material that holds joints together

metabolism chemical processes in your body that turn food into energy

mineral simple substance found naturally in the Earth

negative depressed and downbeat

nicotine poisonous drug found in tobacco

obese very overweight

obsessed think about something all the time

osteoporosis condition that makes bones brittle and fragile

oxygen gas found in the air that humans need to survive

physiotherapist medical person who helps people's bodies recover after illness or injury

professional doing something as a job, not just as a hobby

puberty changes that happen to young people as they grow into adults

qualified having the correct training

stamina when you can exercise for a long time without stopping for a rest

stressed feeling pressured about something

stroke when the blood flow to part of the brain is blocked

supple easy to bend

survive able to live

tar brown substance that contains poisons like arsenic

tendons very strong bands of tissue that connect your muscles to your bones

tension feeling worried and unable to relax

toned muscles are tight and move easily

warm down allows the body to gradually return to its normal activity levels

warm up gradually more energetic activities that safely prepare the body for exercise

weight-bearing exercise exercise that requires the body to carry (bear) its own weight

Index